"We'll help, too!" say Lisa and Ben.

At the , Mr. Green says, "Thanks, kids. Let's move the animals to my house. They can stay there for a few days."

"I love animals," says Ben. "Let's get started!"

"I like furry animals," says Lisa, "but not reptiles. They're creepy! Are there in the ?"

"Let's move the 🐕 first," says Mr. Green.

"My 🚚 can hold 6 big 🗲 on each side.

That's 2 rows of 6 🗲 ."

"6 plus 6 makes 12. Right?" asks Michael.

"That's perfect," says Ben. "There are 12

🐕 in the 🏪 . I love 🐕 . I wish I had

12 of them!"

Ben's dog Noodle barks and runs in a circle.

Lisa takes some 📸 and laughs. "Maybe you

should stick with just one."

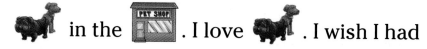

6 + 6 = 12

"We'll need snacks for the 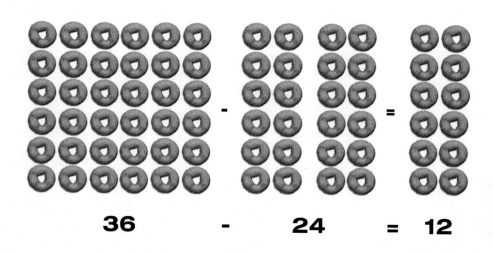, too," Mr.

Green says. "Let's give 2 to each dog."

"12 times 2 is 24," Ben says.

Lisa asks, "Will one be enough?"

Michael reads the . "It has 36 . That's

plenty!"

Lisa nods. "36 minus 24 leaves 12 .

That's 1 extra treat for each dog."

36   -   24   =   12

"The cat 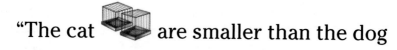 are smaller than the dog

,” Mr. Green says. “And we can put 2

in each cage.”

Lisa says, “7 with 2 in each makes

14 .”

“Right,” says Michael. “That’s 2+2+2+2+2+2+2!”

2 + 2 + 2 + 2 + 2 + 2 + 2 = 14

"Look at the and ," Lisa says.

"They're cute!"

"I'd love to own some ," says Michael.

"They're cool!"

"I think I'd rather take their than clean their ," says Lisa with a smile.

Ben pats Noodle's head. "I'm glad I have my dog."

"Now the 🐰 and 🐭 are safe. Next, let's

move the 🦎 and 🐍 ," Mr. Green says.

Lisa turns pale. " 🦎 and 🐍 ?"

"Yes, and we'll have to be careful with their

glass cases," says Mr. Green.

"I can't move 🦎 and 🐍 ," says Lisa. "No

way!"

Mr. Green smiles. "That's only because you

don't know them yet."

"I used to be afraid of ," Ben says. "Now

I love them—especially Noodle!"

Mr. Green says, "You don't have to move the

and if you don't want to, Lisa."

"Maybe you should take of them," says

Michael. "That way you can get to know

them."

"I'll try. Smile!" Lisa tells an . Then she

says, "Up close, this looks friendly."

Ben laughs. "An is harmless. It eats

, not people."

"Look!" says Lisa. "The escaped! It's in the street!"

"Help!" says Mr. Green.

Lisa runs after the .

"Look out for !" cries Michael.

Lisa grabs the . "Got you," she says,

"just in time."

"You saved him!" Michael says.

Lisa laughs. "He is kind of sweet."

Mr. Green says, "That is yours, if you

want him."

"Thank you!" says Lisa. "He's the

cutest in the world!"

"All the animals are safe now," says Mr. Green.

"Thank you very much!"

"You took a lot of today, Lisa," asks

Michael. "What will you do with them?"

"I want to write about the pet rescue," says

Lisa. "The will make a great story in the

school ."

Mr. Green says, "This story will be good for

my . Thanks again, kids."

"Everyone is happy!" says Ben. "Noodle has a

free biscuit. Lisa has her . Michael has

two ."

"And if those 2 have 6 babies, I'll have 8

," Michael says. "And if some of those

new have babies . . ."

Lisa says, "You'll be cleaning lots of !"

And everyone laughs.

2 + 6 = 8

Did you spot all the picture clues in this
Cheerios reader?

Each picture clue is on a flash card.
Ask a grown-up to cut out the flash cards.
Then try reading the words on the back of
the cards. The pictures will be your clue.

Reading and math are fun with Cheerios!

Just for fun!
Can you find a hidden Cheerio in each picture
in the story?

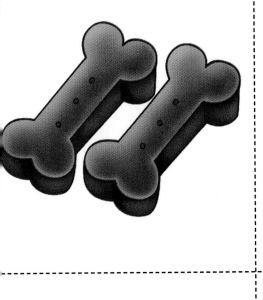

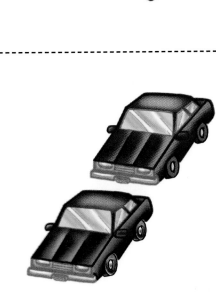

box	biscuits
cages	bugs
cars	cans

dogs	cats
lizards	iguana
newspaper	mice

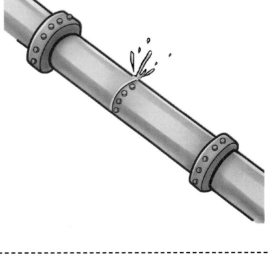

PET SHOP

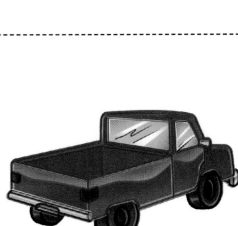

pipe

pictures

pet shop

rabbits

truck

snakes